C is for Contents

A is for Author

Tonee White began quilting five and a half years ago because she wanted quilts to decorate her home. Like many compulsive quilters, she was bitten by the quilting bug during her first class.

Two years later, Tonee began designing and teaching. As she created quilt designs for her home, she offered classes to her friends. Her students encouraged Tonee to send her designs to That Patchwork Place, and the rest, as they say, is history. This book, Tonee's third, is her favorite.

Tonee lives in Irvine, California, with her husband, Bob, and four of her seven children. She thoroughly enjoys one granddaughter, to whom this book is dedicated, and anxiously awaits the arrival of three more grandchildren, including identical twin girls.

Tonee continues to teach and lecture and is currently working on her fourth book.

I is for Introduction

Alphabets are the basis for all written communication; they are at the very core of expression. It's no wonder that we see letters designed in so many ways and that, like all things familiar, we take them for granted.

I have many fond childhood memories, and a strong one is driving coast to coast to visit relatives, playing alphabet games to make time pass more quickly. Quilting seems to evoke childhood memories more than any other thing I do, so creating a quilted alphabet seems a natural progression of my quilting life.

This book includes at least one block pattern for each letter of the alphabet. There are two designs for letters that are frequently used twice in the same word, but I am certain that I have not covered everything. This is an opportunity for you to design letters for yourself. For example, if you notice that your combination of letters evokes a theme, but one of the Alphabet blocks doesn't fit in, go to your dictionary and look for words that begin with the letter you need. I'll bet you find an idea that suits you.

The appliqué patterns I used are simple drawings. It is easy to create your own; inspiration is all around you. Try looking in newspapers, catalogs, children's picture books, cookbooks, and of course, children's coloring books. Your world is full of designs. You just might have to change your way of "looking" to find them.

Be sure to read "D is for Directions" on pages 6–16 thoroughly before beginning a project. The information in this section is not repeated in the patterns for individual Alphabet blocks. Instead, the patterns include special instructions, if needed, for each block; cutting plans for the background; templates for the appliqué pieces; transfer patterns for embroidery; and sources for embellishments. Once you thoroughly understand the general directions, the patterns for each Alphabet block will make sense to you.

There are many ways to use Alphabet blocks and many reasons to make them. I don't think there is a nicer gift than something that has been handmade just for you. These personalized wall hangings make a special present for any occasion. Holiday and theme alphabet designs are already dancing in my head, and some have found their way onto my sketch pads. Let your imagination rise to any occasion, special event, or special person. The possibilities are endless. What fun you'll have!

As I began this project, the ideas flowed profusely, and unlike other projects, although I'm nearing the end of the creative phase, the ideas keep coming. I don't believe the quilted alphabet will ever end for me. This book has been a true "labor of love." I hope it evokes your creativity and that you use it as a "jump start" for creating your own personalized alphabet designs.

D is for Directions

Choosing Fabric and Supplies

Fabric

Other than designing each letter, the most fun I had with this alphabet was choosing the fabric. Here is an opportunity to use up all those scraps you were saving, or to use a small piece of fabric you bought because you loved it but didn't know what to do with it. You can get rid of so much guilt for hoarding and buying!

Each Alphabet block is like a miniquilt. The blocks use as many, if not more, different fabrics than a traditional-size quilt. I selected fabric for each Alphabet block after I designed it. I then cut and sewed the background pieces together and quilted the appliqué pieces to the block.

The subject of the Alphabet block sometimes dictated my fabric color choice. If you want your wall hanging to coordinate with the color scheme of a room or your blocks to coordinate with each other, be a little whimsical. Why not make a purple hand or a yellow tomato? You can get the coordinating effect you want by using the same fabric and/or colors for the borders. Experiment, and above all, have fun!

You won't find yardage amounts or a traditional supply list for these Alphabet blocks. The yardage requirements for each block are so small they aren't worth mentioning. A healthy scrap bag or small amounts of fabrics you love will do just fine.

Recipe for Tea Dyeing

Use this recipe to "age" individual pieces of fabric or an entire block.

1 quart hot tap water
3 tablespoons instant coffee
8 tea bags

Stir instant coffee into water. Let the tea bags steep in the mixture for a few minutes; remove tea bags and soak prewashed fabric in the tea dye for twenty minutes. Soak longer or even overnight to get darker results. To get a blotchy effect, leave the tea bags in the water with the fabric.

Thread

I prefer #8 perle cotton for appliquilt stitching. It is tightly twisted and pulls easily through all three layers of the quilt. My second choice is three or four strands of embroidery floss. Some colors seem to have thicker strands than others, so you may want to experiment.

When I use embroidery floss instead of perle cotton it is for color. There are at least three times as many colors of embroidery floss as there are of perle cotton. Many of my students use embroidery floss because it is easier to find and less expensive than perle cotton. Most who try the perle cotton, however, prefer it to embroidery floss. The strands of embroidery floss sometimes separate, while the tightly twisted strands of perle cotton do not and are easier to pull through the quilt.

Both perle cotton and embroidery floss are much thicker than ordinary thread and, when used in a color that contrasts with the fabric, give quilts the primitive look I am so fond of. However, you can use any type of thread.

I use a contrasting color of perle cotton or embroidery floss in most cases. If your project is mainly pink and blue, use those colors. Stitch the pink appliqué pieces with blue and the blue appliqué pieces with pink. If, however, the piece is small—such as an eye or a small letter—match the color of the thread to the color of the fabric. This way, the small piece is less likely to get lost in the overall design.

It is not necessary to have many different colors of thread. Ecru, medium gray, medium taupe, and black are good colors to start with. Go on to the primary colors from there. Think of a child's box of eight crayons. Children create everything under the sun with those colors, and so can you.

Needles

No matter what the craft or project, I always use the smallest possible needle I can get away with. I prefer a size 6 or size 7 embroidery needle for appliquilt stitching. By flattening the perle cotton or strands of embroidery floss as I moisten the end, I get the end through the needle.

The smaller the needle, the easier it is to pull through the layers of the quilt. The easier the task, the more enjoyable it is. It is important to me that you enjoy appliquilting!

Pinking Shears

My students frequently ask what type of scissors I use. I use three different pairs of pinking shears: Gingher® sawtooth-blade shears, Wiss® scallop-blade shears, and Clover® wave-blade shears. Pinking shears take a bigger bite out of fabric than scissors, but they make a nicer edge on appliqué pieces and limit fraying.

I use the Clover wave-blade pinking shears most often because they take a smaller bite than the other two shears. The larger the bite, the less detail you have on your appliqué piece. In the majority of my Appliquilt designs, precise detail is not necessary to recognize the object. But since most of the appliqué pieces in the Alphabet blocks are small, I used my Clover shears almost exclusively.

Rotary Cutters, Mats, and Rulers

The speed and efficiency with which you can rotary-cut fabric is truly one of the seven wonders of my life. I will never forget my amazement when this was demonstrated to me for the first time. Luckily, wave- and pinking-edge rotary-cutter blades are now available. I use these blades and wholeheartedly recommend them for cutting binding and larger appliqué pieces.

When rotary cutting, use a mat so you don't damage the cutting surface or dull your blade.

Another necessary rotary-cutting tool is an acrylic ruler. I have many rulers, and I use them all. They really do make accurate cutting a breeze. I particularly recommend the larger rulers, such as the 12½" and 15" squares. They are indispensable for cutting background patches. I find rulers to be much more accurate than using the grid on a mat. I do, however, measure fabric with the mat grid if my rulers are not large enough to do the job.

Template Plastic and Pencils

I almost always use template plastic for transferring designs from paper to fabric. The firm edge allows me to make more accurate lines. Plastic templates also last longer because they do not bend or tear. I may use the same template on different projects; therefore, I prefer the permanency a heavyweight plastic provides. I

find that flat sheets of template plastic are much easier to use and store than rolled sheets.

I use a soft #2 lead pencil for marking on light- or medium-colored fabric. On dark fabric, I use a white or pastel chalk pencil. If you trace the appliqué pieces on the wrong side of the fabric, you don't need to worry about lines showing on your finished piece.

Batting

I have always used Pellon™ fleece in my Appliquilt projects because it is easy to stitch through. However, I used a lightweight cotton/polyester (80/20) batting for these Alphabet blocks. Initially, I used this batting because I had so many scraps and scraps work well in these blocks. I found that this batting works better than the Pellon fleece because it is heavier and better supports the embellishments. Of course, any type of batting will do. My only suggestion is that if you use different types of batting, try to use types with the same thickness in all your blocks.

Constructing Alphabet Blocks

Each Alphabet block measures 8½" x 8½" when finished. The blocks are pieced, layered, and appliquilted. They are not bound. The instructions for each block include a cutting plan that shows the measurement of each piece. **All measurements include ¼"-wide seam allowances.**

The background pieces are **numbered** to show the stitching order. Stitch the pieces together in numerical order until you have completed a 6½" square. For most of the blocks, this is the approximate size before the borders are added.

Do not be concerned if at this point you do not have an exact 6½" square. Fabrics stretch and give as you sew them, and the number of seams made in either direction can also affect the final measurement. As long as your square measures approximately 6½" you will be fine. If you want your block to be exactly 8½" square, however, this is the time to trim.

In the cutting plan for each block, the borders are **lettered** to show the stitching order. Stitch each border (top, right side, bottom, and left side) to the 6½" square, beginning with *A* and ending with *D*. You must piece some of the borders. These borders have a letter and a number; for instance, *A1*.

I pieced all my blocks by machine, using twelve stitches per inch and a ¼"-wide seam allowance. Make each seam as straight as you can. Press well after sewing each seam.

Making the Appliquilt Sandwich

Cut a square, 10" x 10", from your batting and backing fabric. Your block top will "creep" out a bit as you quilt it, and this gives you plenty of room. Layer the top on the batting and backing. Smooth it well and pin the layers together.

Using perle cotton, stitch around each patch ¼" in from the seam. You are now ready to stitch on the appliqué pieces.

Cutting Out Appliqué Pieces

Trace the templates onto template plastic or paper. As mentioned earlier, I prefer plastic because it provides a firm edge to trace around when transferring the shape to fabric. However, a paper template will do.

After cutting out your template, trace around it on the wrong side of the fabric. I recommend that you trace on the wrong side of the fabric so that, when you cut out your appliqué piece, no lines show on the finished piece. If you use light fabric, a soft #2 lead pencil works well. If you use a dark fabric, you may need to use a white or pastel chalk pencil.

Turn the template over so that the right side of the template is face down on the wrong side of the fabric; then trace around it.

The direction of the template is not crucial for many of the designs. For instance, the hand on the H is for Hand block works well either way, while the *N* on the I is for Ink block really needs to be reversed.

Using pinking shears, cut out the appliqué pieces on the drawn lines. You do not need to add seam allowances, because nothing is turned under.

Your appliqué pieces are now ready to place on your Alphabet block. If the pieces do not lie flat, now is the time to press them.

The numbers on some of the templates indicate stitching order.

Learning to Appliquilt

The stitching is the most important ingredient in an Appliquilt, and happily, it is the easiest to do. I call this stitching "my therapy." It calms me right down after a stressful hour or even a stressful day.

It is important for you to relax and have fun. Don't worry about the size and uniformity of your stitches. The larger and more uneven they are, the more primitive your piece will look. Don't bury those knots in the batting. Allow them to sit proudly on top for all to see.

Start stitching on the top side of your quilt, leaving a 6"-long tail. Using a simple running or basting stitch, sew through all the layers.

Running Stitch

When stitching around an appliqué piece, work your way back to where you started. End the stitching on the top and tie the two ends together in a square knot (right over left and left over right). Clip the ends to whatever length you like. I usually leave a ¼"-long tail.

Starting point— leave 6"-long tail.

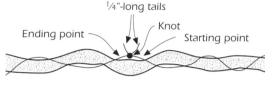

¼"-long tails

Ending point   Knot   Starting point

Knot and trim to ¼"-long tails.

If you run out of perle cotton or embroidery floss, end your stitching on top and leave a 6"-long tail. Start stitching where you ended, leaving another 6"-long tail. After taking a few stitches, tie the two tails together in a square knot.

If you begin stitching at a point that you will not stitch back to, tie a knot in the end of the thread before you begin. Start your stitching on the top of your project. When you come to the end of the stitching, gather the last few stitches ever so slightly. Make a loop with the thread and put your needle through the loop with the tip of the needle resting on the spot where the knot will be. Pull the loop to tighten the knot to the point where the tip of your needle lies. Your knot should sit snugly against the fabric when you smooth the gathers.

Using Embroidery

You may want to embroider the Alphabet blocks' lettering and designs, such as the sun's rays on the F is for Farm block and the rain lines on the U is for Umbrella block. Use a transfer pen to transfer designs to fabric. First trace the design onto white paper with a pencil. Turn the paper over and place it on a light source, such as a window or light box. Trace over the image with the transfer pen. Iron the image onto the block in the appropriate place.

Transfer pens are available in white for use with dark fabrics and in black for use with light fabrics. Follow the manufacturer's directions for whatever pen you choose.

You don't have to limit yourself to the designs in this book. I encourage you to draw your own designs and use your handwriting to personalize your Appliquilt projects. Use a white or pastel pencil on dark fabrics and a lead pencil on lighter fabrics.

Three or four strands of embroidery floss work well to cover the drawn or transferred images. I use a backstitch for lines, and make dots, such as for the letter *i*, with French knots.

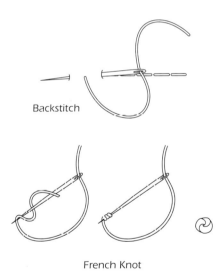

Backstitch

French Knot

You may do the embroidery before or after you make the appliquilt sandwich. If you choose to do it after, simply run your needle through the batting as you stitch. Begin from the back and tie off on the back.

Embellishing Your Blocks

The embellishments used on these little quilts are what "make" them. Without all the buttons, pieces of jute, bits of lace, and miniatures, these Alphabet blocks would lack a great deal of their appeal. I embellish most of my projects using a "planned scatter" method. That is, I plan the placement to make it look scattered. Everything should be asymmetrical, but balanced.

To attach buttons, start on the top of the block and leave a 6"-long tail. Stitch through the button once. Tie off on the top using a square knot. Clip the ends, leaving little tails.

When attaching an embellishment that does not have holes, cut a 12"-long piece of perle cotton (or some heavier medium you can thread through a needle). Using epoxy glue, attach the midpoint of the perle cotton to the back of the object. Thread one end of the perle cotton through the needle and run it through the block to the back. Do the same with the other end. Tie the two ends together in a triple knot on the back and bury the ends in the batting. This method also works well for embellishments that have a loop or only one hole.

See "Resources" on page 21 to find sources for many of the embellishments I used in my blocks.

Making Yo-Yos

Yo-yos are wonderful design elements and are easy to make the Appliquilt way.

To make a yo-yo:

1. Trace the circular pattern for the yo-yo on the wrong side of the fabric. Cut out the circle with pinking shears.
2. Thread a needle, using an 18" length of perle cotton or embroidery floss. Make a knot 4" from the end of the thread.
3. With the right side of the fabric facing you, stitch around the circle, ¼" in from the outer edge. Gather fabric against the knot as you stitch.
4. When you have stitched entirely around the circle, adjust the gathers. Do not pull the gathers together entirely. I leave a center hole about the size of my index finger. Tie the thread in a square knot with the tail you left when you began. Flatten the yo-yo so that the hole is in the center of the circle. Do not trim the thread tails.

5. Position the yo-yo on the Alphabet block. With the thread still in the needle, stitch a button over the hole. End the stitching on the top of the block. Tie the tails in a knot and trim.

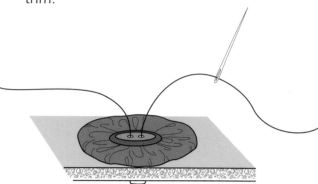

You can also run the thread through the hole, between the layers, and out through the folded edge of the yo-yo. Stitch the yo-yo to the Alphabet block with a running stitch or blind hemstitch with the gathered side facing up or down. If you use this approach, it is best to tie off on the back.

Finishing Alphabet Blocks

After you've finished stitching and embellishing your Alphabet block, trim the excess batting and backing fabric even with the top. I use my rotary cutter, but straight scissors or pinking shears also work well.

If you plan to hang your blocks on a button foundation (pages 13–16), attach loops to the top corners of the block. Simply cut a piece of jute, ribbon, or string approximately 3" long. Machine stitch both ends to a corner. Cover the ends of the loop and the stitches with a button or other embellishment.

Building the Button Foundation

After designing a few Alphabet blocks and making them into miniquilts, the practical side of me kept saying, "What are you going to do with these cute letters?" So I came up with the idea of using them to spell out names, of course, and to make a foundation with buttons on it for attaching the miniquilts. With a button foundation, you can change the name to fit the occasion or even change the occasion. If there is a birthday, attach the Birthday block in the border and spell out the birthday person's name. If someone got a great report card or a promotion, put the Good for You block in the border. If you don't have a particular occasion to herald, put the House block in the border and spell out the family name. I'm sure you will think of more Occasion blocks (I know I have), and I hope you design and construct them.

You can also make quilts based on a theme. For example, words such as "farm" and "quilts" are fun. If you have a soccer player in the family, you might want to spell out the word "soccer." The word "teacher" is another possibility, whether it applies to you or as a gift for a particularly inspiring person. There are a lot of wonderful people who are not given enough recognition for the good work they do.

A great way for children to learn the alphabet is to live with it in their rooms and become familiar with the letters as they learn to talk, associating letters with familiar objects. I designed this alphabet with children in mind. I tried to keep the symbols simple and easily recognizable.

Using Alphabet blocks as teaching tools makes learning the alphabet fun. What a wonderful gift for any child or teacher! Here's a way for you to contribute to that knowledge and to create an heirloom.

Have fun with the button foundations. The borders are like a blank canvas, and you can say or draw whatever you like. I have used these spaces for my favorite traditional blocks, sayings that compliment the theme, or whatever I think goes well with the thought I'm conveying with the letters.

However, you may not want to get too flamboyant. There is a lot going on in the letters, and you may not want the button foundation to detract from them. If you do have a lot planned for your foundation, use quieter, small prints or solids for the letters. If you really have something to shout about, there should be no limits put on your imagination and creativity.

If you think the word or name says it all, make a narrower border in a simple print or solid color. These Alphabet blocks stand on their own quite nicely.

Determining the Size of the Background

The most difficult part of making the button foundation is determining the size you want. There are several ways to figure this out: use the longest name in your family, the longest word that you might want to spell, or the space in which you will hang the foundation.

Once you know the number of Alphabet blocks you want to use, measure a few of your blocks.

1. Take the average width measurement (it should be approximately 8½") and multiply it by the number of Alphabet blocks you want to use.

2. Add 1" per Alphabet block for the spacing between each letter and the borders. For example, 8½" multiplied by 6 blocks equals 51". Add 6" (1" for each block) for a total of 57". This is the width for the button foundation background, without borders.

3. Add 1" to the height of your Alphabet blocks. If the blocks are 8½" square, they are 8½" high. Therefore, the background would be 9½" high.

4. Add ½" for seam allowances. In the example given, the background piece would be at least 10" x 57½".

Determining the Size of the Borders

If you want to add borders, you need to have a pretty good idea of what you plan to put in them. The Occasion blocks included in this book are 3" to 4" high. If you plan to use these and/or develop some of your own, the top border should be 3" to 4" high. This does not mean that all the borders must be this height. Use your creativity and make this quilt your own.

The borders of "The Whites" on pages 18–19 are different sizes. The top and left side borders are 4½" wide, but the right border is 2½" wide and the bottom border is 1½" wide.

To determine the size of borders:

1. Cut the top and bottom borders the same width as the pieced background.

2. For the right and left borders, add the height of the top and bottom borders to the height of the background, then subtract the seam allowance. For example, if you wanted the finished height of the top and bottom borders to be 3" each, you would add 7" (6" plus the seam allowance) to the 10" background measurement. After you subtracted the seam allowance, you would cut the right and left borders 16".

Assembling the Button Foundation

All seam allowances are ¼" wide.

1. Cut the batting and backing fabric approximately 4" larger than the pieced top so the top has room to creep out a little during construction. Add the cut measurements of the background and borders, subtract the seam allowances, and add 4".

2. Lay the backing fabric, right side down, on a flat surface such as a floor or large table. Tape the opposing edges to the surface using 2"-wide tape (or clamps if using a table).

3. Lay the batting on top of the backing fabric, smoothing it from the center out. Match the edges of the batting with the backing fabric.

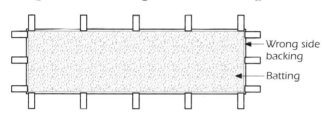

Wrong side backing
Batting

4. Place the top in the center of the batting, right side up, again smoothing from the center out. Starting at the center, pin approximately every 6" as shown. Remove the tape.

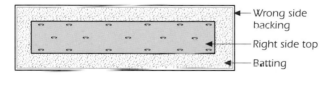

Wrong side backing
Right side top
Batting

5. Lay the top border on top of the background, right sides together, matching upper edges. Pin in place.

6. Using a ¼"-wide seam allowance, stitch through all the layers.

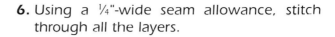

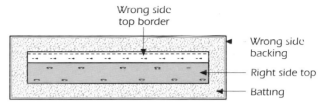

Wrong side top border
Wrong side backing
Right side top
Batting

Use a ¼"-wide seam allowance.

7. Remove the pins placed in step 5 and flip the border right side up onto the batting. Press the seam.

8. Repeat this procedure for the bottom border.

9. With right sides together, pin the right border on top of the background. The right border should cover the top and bottom borders.

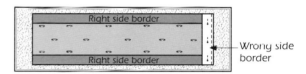

Right side border
Right side border
Wrong side border

Use a ¼"-wide seam allowance.

10. Stitch through all the layers. Remove the pins placed in step 9 and flip the border right side up onto the batting. Press the seam.

11. Repeat this procedure for the left border.

Binding the Button Foundation

Cut 1¼"- to 1½"-wide binding strips with pinking shears or the pinking blade on your rotary cutter. Fold the strips in half lengthwise and, with the wrong sides together, press. After trimming the batting and backing to match the quilt top, wrap the binding strip around the edge of the quilt. Match the crease edge with the edge of the quilt and pin at the beginning and 6" to 8" from the first pin.

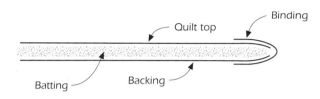

When you need to add another binding strip, simply overlap the ends of the binding strips 1". I usually take two stitches where the binding strips overlap. This eliminates the need to sew binding strips together before you begin.

I arrange and pin the binding 10" to 12" ahead of my stitching. I do not pin all the way around the quilt. This eliminates pins that may scratch or prick me while I'm stitching.

Start stitching approximately 1" from the end of the binding strip. Using perle cotton, stitch about ¼" from the inside edge of the binding. Stitch through all the layers. Use the same running stitch you use for appliquilting.

Miter the corners as you approach them by folding and pinning. I take two stitches in the corners to secure the folds. Check the back of the quilt to make sure you catch the fold of the miters on the back as well as the front.

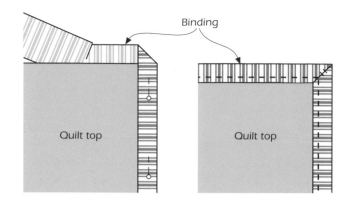

This binding method looks good with the button foundations. However, if you have a favorite method you prefer, feel free to use it.

Adding Buttons

Your foundation is now ready for buttons. Don't feel the buttons have to match. Different colors and designs add to the primitive look. Just be sure the buttons are the right size for the loops you put on the letters.

I use perle cotton or embroidery floss to attach buttons.

1. Arrange your Alphabet blocks on the foundation. Place a pin in the foundation at the upper corner of each block.

2. Sew a button to the foundation where you placed your pins. Start on the top of the button. Run the thread through the button and all the layers of the foundation, leaving a 6"-long tail.

3. Stitch through all the button holes at least once, ending on the top of the button foundation.

4. Using a square knot (page 10), tie the thread off with the tail you left at the beginning. Trim the thread ends.

G is for Gallery

"Now I Know My A Bee Zzzz" by Tonee White, 1994, Irvine, California, 62" x 54".
What a wonderful gift for any child or teacher!

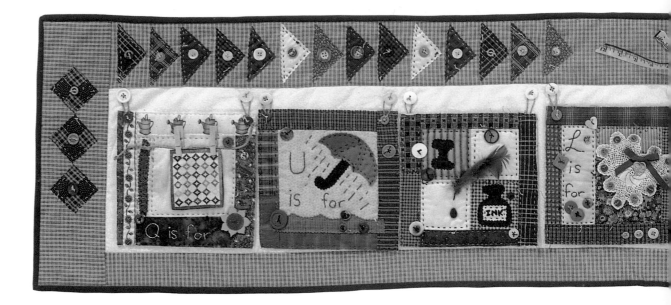

"Kerry" by Tonee White, 1994,
Irvine, California, 18" x 51½".
What a wonderful way to
tell someone that you
appreciate them.

"Quilt" by Tonee White, 1994,
Irvine, California, 16" x 58½".
Sew many possibilities!

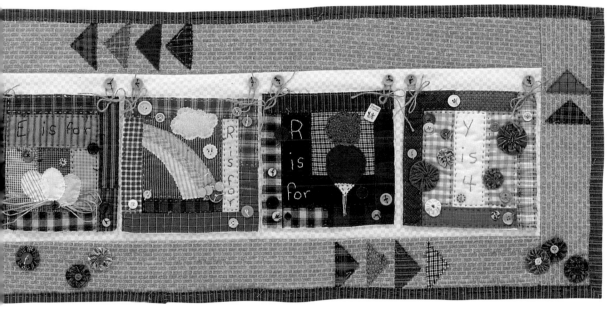

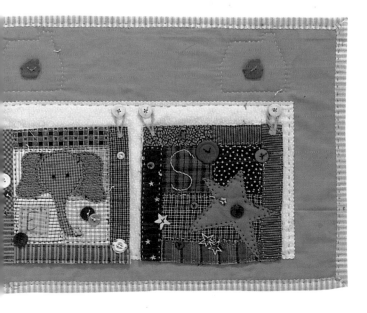

"The Whites" by Tonee White, 1994,
Irvine, California, 17" x 64".
Celebrate a special occasion or spell
out a family name. The borders are
like a blank canvas, and you can say
or draw whatever you like.

"Dad" by Tonee White, 1994, Irvine, California, 17½" x 35".
This quilt makes a special gift for a particularly inspiring person!

"Farm" by Tonee White, 1994, Irvine, California, 17½" x 43".
This is a fun use for all those great farm-theme fabrics.

R is for Resources

Tools

Clover
For store locations, call 1-800-233-1703

Stencils

Country Stencils
1534 Marsetta Drive
Beavercreek, Ohio 45432

Rubber Stamps

Stampa Barbara
505 Paseo Nuevo
Santa Barbara, California 93101

Embellishments

Apple Creek
3004 Glenfield Lane
Ceres, California 95307

Dogwood Lane
Box 145
Dugger, IN 47848

A Homespun Heart
2223 F Street
Iowa City, Iowa 52245

Ann Shafer
11952 Norma Lane
Garden Grove, California 92640

Sugar Babies
1435 Salvador Circle
Corona, California 91720

P is for Patterns

Refer to "D is for Directions" on pages 6–16 as you construct your blocks. All the blocks are made in the same basic manner. The following patterns include special instructions, if needed, for each block; cutting plans for the background; templates for the appliqué pieces; transfer patterns for embroidery; and sources for embellishments.

I offer these designs as suggestions and inspirations; use your creativity and make them your own.

A is for Angel

A is for Angel Cutting Plan

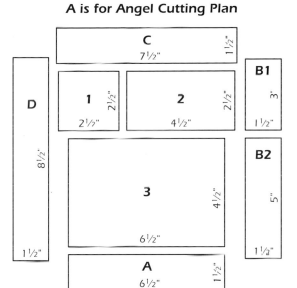

Color photo on page 41

The measurements shown include ¼"-wide seam allowances.

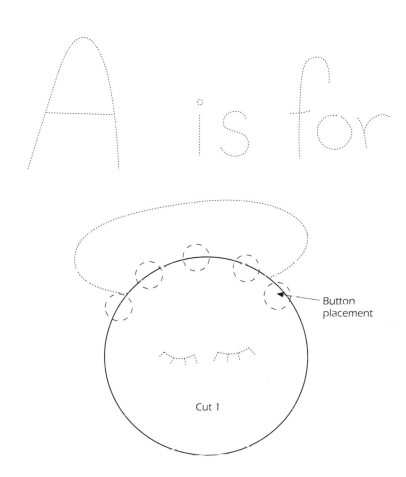

Button placement

Cut 1

1. Using pinking shears, cut a 4" x 6" rectangle of fabric for the angel's wings. Stitch down the center of the fabric rectangle. Gather your stitching to 1½". Position the wings 1" above the bottom border. Stitch down the center through all the layers.

2. Stitch the angel's face over the gathers. Refer to the block illustration for placement.
3. Using six strands of embroidery floss, embroider the angel's halo and eyelashes.
The gold and silver nailhead stars are available at most fabric stores.

Color
photo
on page
41

A is for Apple Cutting Plan

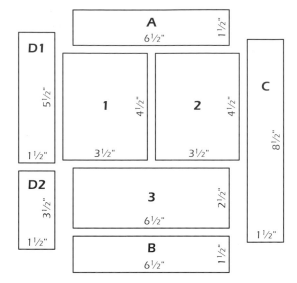

The measurements shown include ¼"-wide seam allowances.

Cut 1

Cut 1

Cut 1

Cut 1

Cutting line → Cut heart shape out of apple.

1. Make templates for the apple and heart. Trace around the apple and heart templates on the wrong side of the fabric.

2. To cut out the heart, use the tip of a small pair of scissors to make a small hole at any point on the traced line. Cut along the line. Refer to the block illustration for placement.

The red apple button is available at most fabric stores. The cinnamon apple button is from Sugar Babies. See "Resources" on page 21.

B is for Barn Cutting Plan

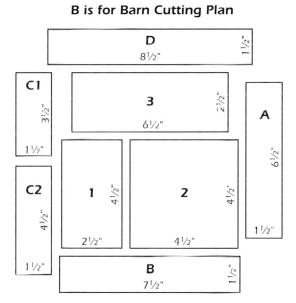

The measurements shown include ¼"-wide seam allowances.

2
Cut 1

1
Cut 1

3
Cut 1

4
Cut 1

This block was fun; it gave me an opportunity to use those great farmyard fabrics that are available. Refer to the block illustration for placement.

1. Cut an 8"- to 9"-long piece of raffia and fold it in ½"- to 1"-long loops.

2. Using invisible nylon thread, machine stitch the raffia to the barn window. Cut the loops and trim the raffia.

The chicken and egg buttons are available from Apple Creek. See "Resources" on page 21.

Color
photo
on page
41

B is for Buttons & Bow Cutting Plan

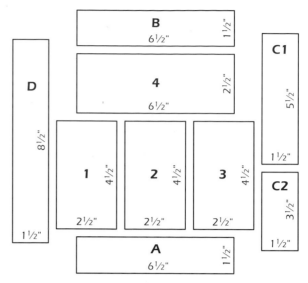

The measurements shown include ¼"-wide seam allowances.

1. Cut a strip of fabric, 1½" x 15", for the bow. I tore this strip to fray the edges. Refer to the block illustration for placement.

2. To attach the bow, take two stitches from the back of the block. Tie the thread tails in a square knot.

3. Embellish with buttons.

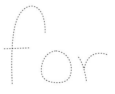

C is for Chicken

C is for Chicken Cutting Plan

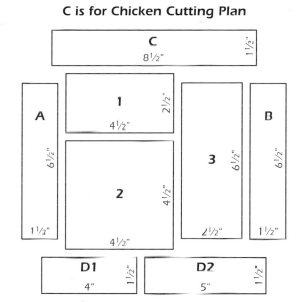

Color photo on page 41

The measurements shown include ¼"-wide seam allowances.

There are no special instructions for this Alphabet block. Refer to the block illustration for placement.

Color
photo
on page
41

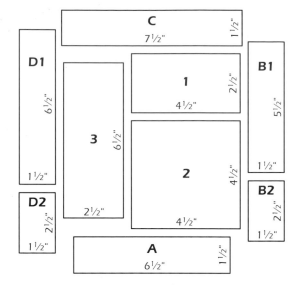

D is for Daisy Cutting Plan

The measurements shown include ¼"-wide seam allowances.

1. Embroider the stem of the daisy.
2. Overlap eight petals at the top of the stem. Stitch the remaining two petals as though they were falling or had fallen from the flower. Refer to the block illustration for placement.

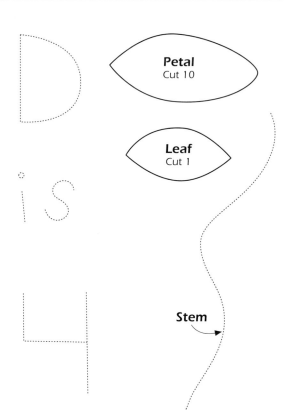

Petal
Cut 10

Leaf
Cut 1

Stem

D is for Dart

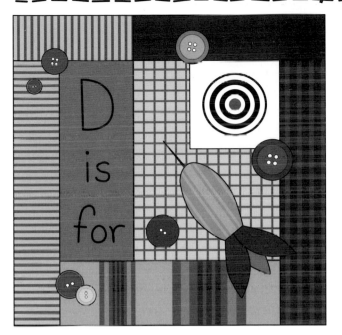

D is for Dart Cutting Plan

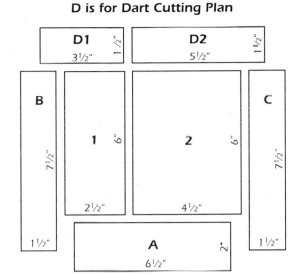

Color photo on page 42

The measurements shown include ¼"-wide seam allowances.

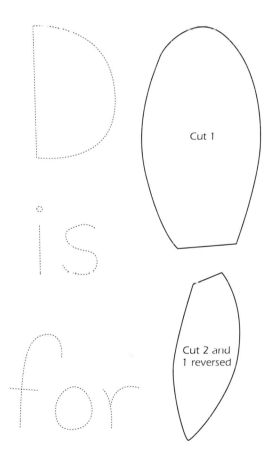

Cut 1

Cut 2 and 1 reversed

1. Make a template for the dart flights. Trace around the template on the wrong side of your fabrics and cut out the appliqué pieces. Use a contrasting fabric for the middle flight.

2. Stitch the dart and middle flight to the block first. Overlap the other two flights on each side and stitch. Refer to the block illustration for placement.

3. To make the target, I used a 2¼" square of tightly woven muslin and stamped it with a target stamp from Stampa Barbara. (See "Resources" on page 21.) I colored in the stamp outline with permanent-ink fabric markers. If you would like more information on using rubber stamps, refer to my first book, *Appliquilt* .

Color
photo
on page
42

D is for Dog Cutting Plan

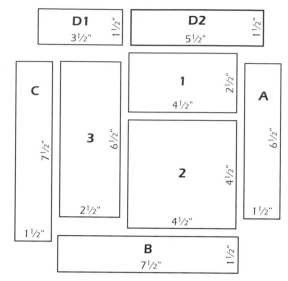

The measurements shown include ¼"-wide seam allowances.

There are no special instructions for this Alphabet block. Refer to the block illustration for placement.

D

is for

1
Cut 1

2
Cut 1

E is for Egg Cutting Plan

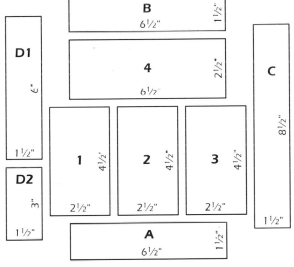

Color photo on page 42

The measurements shown include ¼"-wide seam allowances.

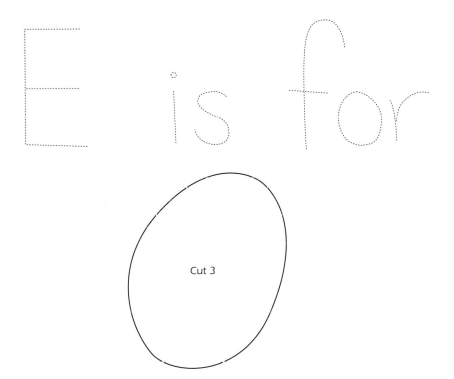

Cut 3

1. Cut a 40"- to 45"-long piece of raffia and fold it in 6"-long loops. Leave an end extending on each side.
2. Position the raffia on your Alphabet block. Refer to the block illustration for placement.
3. Pin the raffia loops to the block through the center of the raffia. Machine stitch the raffia

through the center of the loops.
4. Sew a button in the center of the raffia to hide the stitching.
5. Stitch the right and left egg in place; then stitch the middle egg so that it overlaps the other eggs.

E is for Elephant

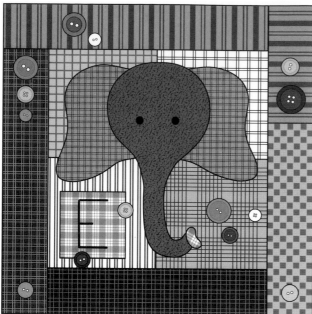

Color photo on page 42

E is for Elephant Cutting Plan

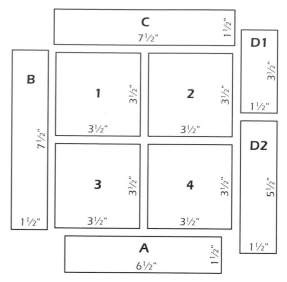

The measurements shown include ¼"-wide seam allowances.

1. Embroider the *E* on a 2" square of fabric, then stitch the square of fabric to the block. Refer to the block illustration for placement.

2. Use small buttons for the elephant's eyes. Refer to the templates for placement.

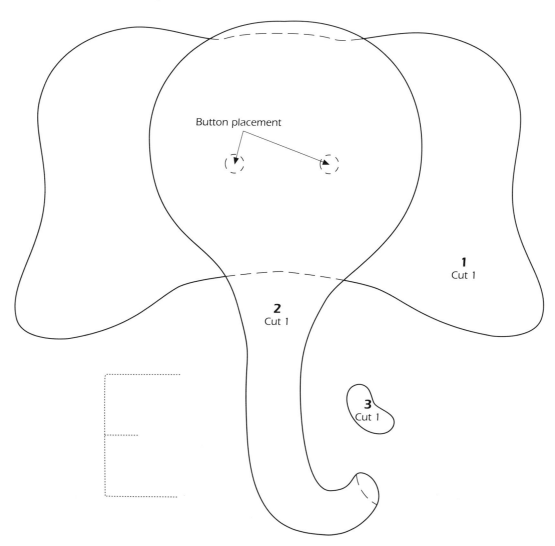

Button placement

1
Cut 1

2
Cut 1

3
Cut 1

F is for Farm

Color photo on page 42

F is for Farm Cutting Plan

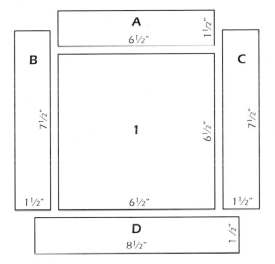

	A 6½" 1½"	
B 7½"	**1** 6½" 6½"	**C** 7½"
1½"	6½"	1½"
	D 8½" ½"	

The measurements shown include ¼"-wide seam allowances

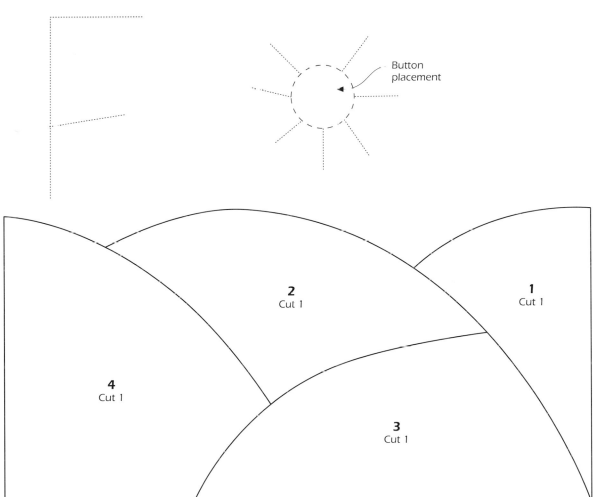

Button placement

2 Cut 1

1 Cut 1

4 Cut 1

3 Cut 1

1. Use contrasting fabrics for the landscape. Cut the appliqué pieces slightly larger than drawn so you can overlap them. Refer to the block illustration for placement.

2. Embroider the *F* and the sun rays with embroidery floss.

The barn, cow, tractor, radish, and corn buttons are from Apple Creek. The cinnamon button is from Sugar Babies. See "Resources" on page 21.

F is for Flag

Color
photo
on page
42

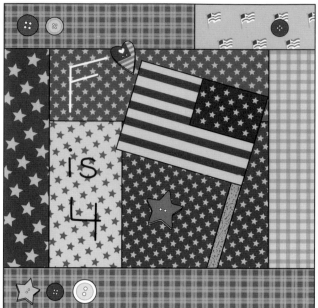

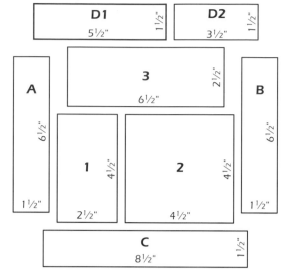

F is for Flag Cutting Plan

D1	1½"	D2	1½"
5½"		3½"	

A		3		B
6½"		6½"	2½"	6½"
1½"	1 (2½")	2 (4½")	4½"	1½"

C	1½"
8½"	

The measurements shown include ¼"-wide seam allowances.

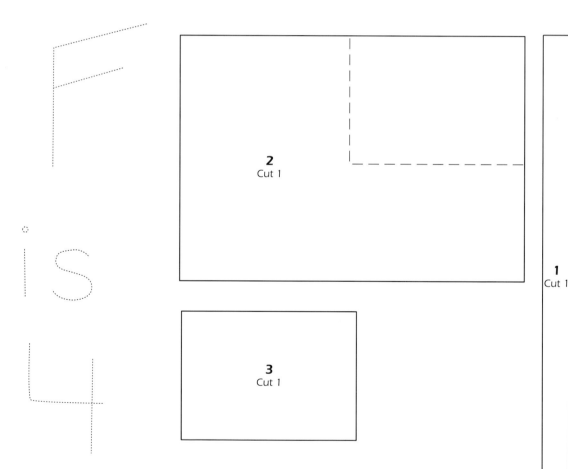

2
Cut 1

1
Cut 1

3
Cut 1

1. I used a preprinted flag for my Alphabet block. You can use a preprinted flag or make a flag. To make a flag, cut a 3½" x 2½" rectangle of striped fabric and a 1¾" x 1¾" square of star or other print fabric (or use the appliqué pieces provided above). Position the rectangle on the block and stitch. Position the square in the upper corner of the rectangle and stitch.

2. Stitch the flagpole and flag pieces to the block. Refer to the block illustration for placement.

The star button is from Apple Creek. The patriotic heart button is from Dogwood Lane. See "Resources" on page 21.

G is for Gingerbread

G is for Gingerbread Cutting Plan

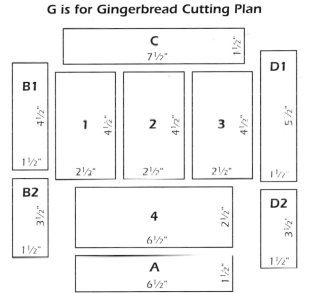

Color photo on page 43

The measurements shown include ¼"-wide seam allowances.

I used brown wool fabric for my gingerbread man. Refer to the block illustration for placement.

The small wooden heart buttons are available at most craft supply shops. The cinnamon heart and gingerbread man buttons are from Sugar Babies. See "Resources" on page 21.

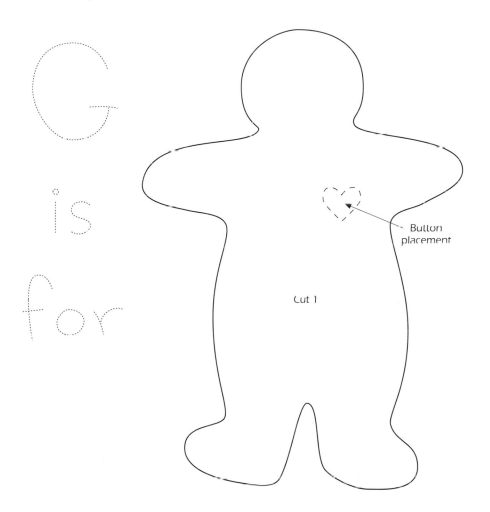

G is for

Cut 1

Button placement

Color photo on page 43

G is for Goose Cutting Plan

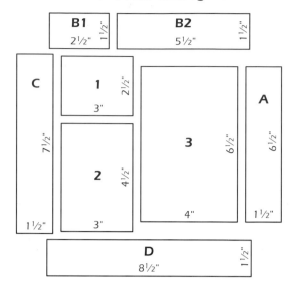

B1 1½" 2½"		**B2** 1½" 5½"

| **C** 7½" 1½" | **1** 2½" 3" | | **A** 6½" 1½" |
| | **2** 4½" 3" | **3** 6½" 4" | |

| **D** 8½" 1½" |

The measurements shown include ¼"-wide seam allowances.

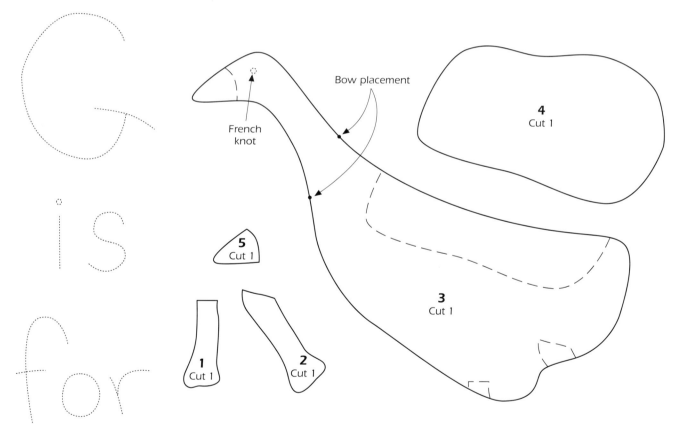

Bow placement

French knot

4 Cut 1

5 Cut 1

3 Cut 1

1 Cut 1

2 Cut 1

1. For the goose's body and wing, cut one appliqué piece from muslin and a second appliqué piece from white flannel. Cut the flannel pieces slightly smaller than the muslin pieces. Layer the two pieces, muslin on top, and stitch to the block. The flannel prevents the background fabric from showing through the muslin. Refer to the block illustration for placement.

2. Cut a 12"-long piece of perle cotton. Refer-

ring to the template, stitch from the top of the block at a point on the goose's neck. Leave a 4"-long tail. Pull the perle cotton back up to the point on the opposite side of the neck.

3. Thread a bead or trinket on the perle cotton and tie a bow, using the thread in your needle and the 4"-long tail.

4. Make a French knot for the goose's eye. See "Using Embroidery" on page 11.

Color
photo
on page
43

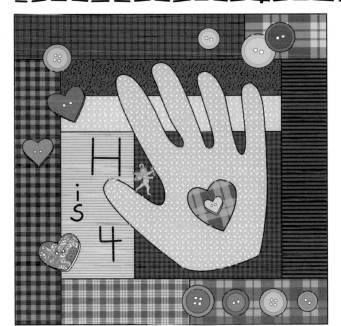

H is for Hand & Heart Cutting Plan

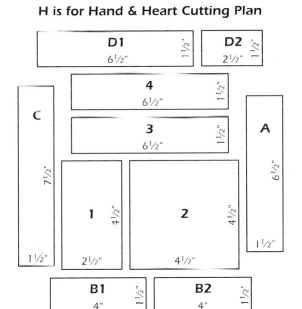

D1 6½"	1½"	**D2** 2½" 1½"

C 7½" 1½"

4 6½" 1½"

3 6½" 1½"

A 6½" 1½"

1 2½" 4½"

2 4½" 4½"

B1 4" 1½"

B2 4" 1½"

The measurements shown include ¼"-wide seam allowances.

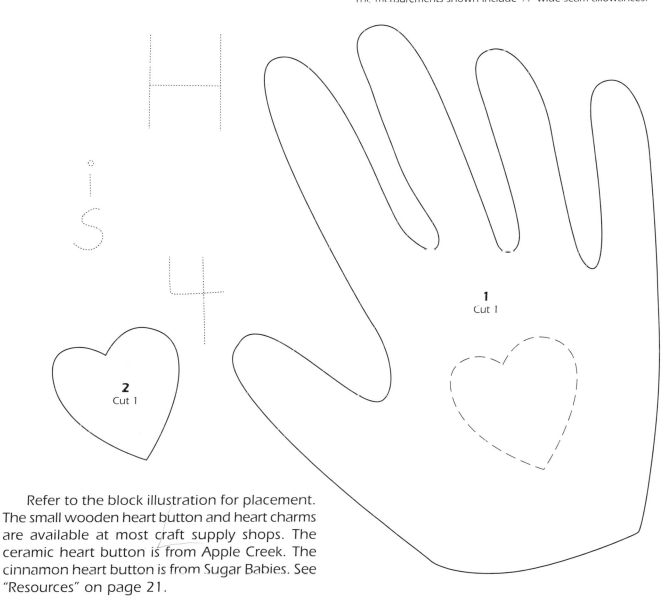

H

i

S

4

1
Cut 1

2
Cut 1

Refer to the block illustration for placement. The small wooden heart button and heart charms are available at most craft supply shops. The ceramic heart button is from Apple Creek. The cinnamon heart button is from Sugar Babies. See "Resources" on page 21.

Color
photo
on page
43

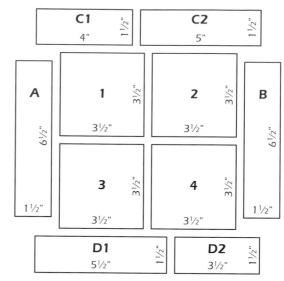

I is for Ink Cutting Plan

C1	C2
4" 1½"	5" 1½"

A	1	2	B
6½"	3½" / 3½"	3½" / 3½"	6½"
1½"			1½"

	3	4	
	3½" / 3½"	3½" / 3½"	

D1	D2
5½" 1½"	3½" 1½"

The measurements shown include ¼"-wide seam allowances.

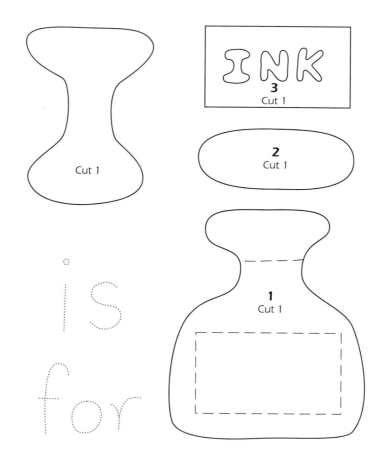

INK 3
Cut 1

2
Cut 1

1
Cut 1

is
for

You need a small piece of fusible web, such as Wonder-Under or HeatnBond™, to add the "INK" pieces this block.

1. Referring to "Cutting Out Appliqué Pieces" on page 9, make appliqué pieces for the *I*, ink jar, lid, label, and "INK."

2. To fuse the word "INK" to the label, follow the manufacturer's instructions for using fusible web. Reverse the letters when tracing on the fusible web. Refer to the block illustration for placement.

Small feathers are usually available at craft supply shops.

J is for Jam

Color photo on page 43

J is for Jam Cutting Plan

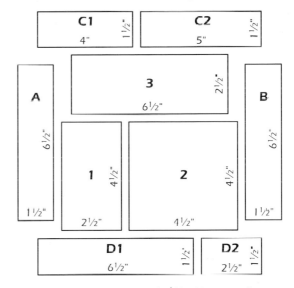

C1	C2
4" 1½"	5" 1½"

A	3	B
6½" 1½"	6½" 2½"	6½" 1½"

1	2
4½"	4½"
2½"	4½"

D1	D2
6½" 1½"	2½" 1½"

The measurements shown include ¼"-wide seam allowances.

1. Referring to "Cutting Out Appliqué Pieces" on page 9, make appliqué pieces for the jar, lid, and label.

2. Using a transfer pen, transfer the word "JAM" to the label. Follow the pen manufacturer's instructions. Embroider the letters or just use the transfer image. Refer to the block illustration for placement.

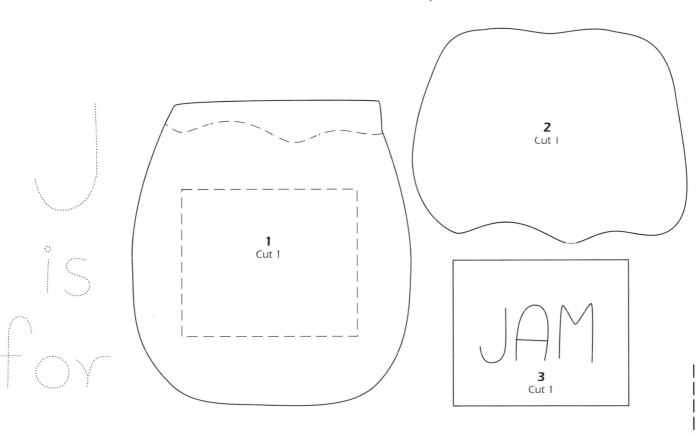

J is for

1
Cut 1

2
Cut 1

JAM

3
Cut 1

Color
photo
on page
43

K is for Key Cutting Plan

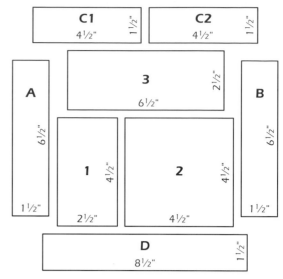

C1		C2	
4½"	1½"	4½"	1½"

A 6½" × 1½" × 2½"

3 — 6½" × 2½"

B 6½" × 1½"

1 — 4½" × 2½"

2 — 4½" × 4½"

D 8½" × 1½"

The measurements shown include ¼"-wide seam allowances.

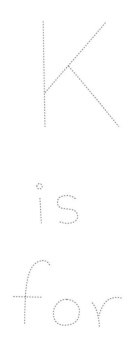

K
is
for

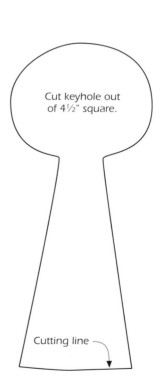

Cut keyhole out
of 4½" square.

Cutting line

1. Use two pieces of fabric for Piece 2. Cut a 4½"
   square of black fabric and a 4½" square of
   fabric for Piece 2.
2. Make a template for the keyhole. Trace around
   the template on the wrong side of the fabric
   for Piece 2.

3. Using pinking shears, cut along the drawn
   line.
4. Place Piece 2 on top of the black 4½" square.
   Line up the edges of the two squares.
5. Sew this set of squares into the block.
   I found the key charm at a craft supply shop.

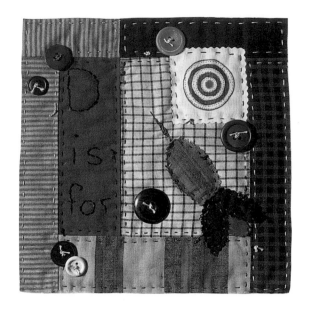

Color photo on page 44

L is for Lace & Love Cutting Plan

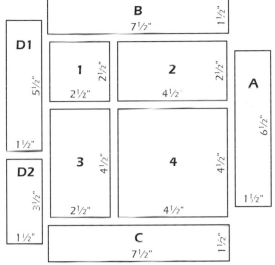

The measurements shown include ¼"-wide seam allowances.

I used a doily for the heart, but you can also use fabric or lace. You can appliquilt your heart to your Alphabet block, or you can tie your heart to the block as I did. Refer to the block illustration for placement.

1. Make a bow from ⅛"-wide satin ribbon. To attach the bow, take two stitches from the back of the block through the center of the bow. Secure the ends with small buttons.

2. Cut a 6"-long strip of lace. Referring to the block illustration for placement, position the strip of lace on your Alphabet block. Attach the lace to the block with buttons.

The lavender heart button is from A Homespun Heart. See "Resources" on page 21.

Color
photo
on page
44

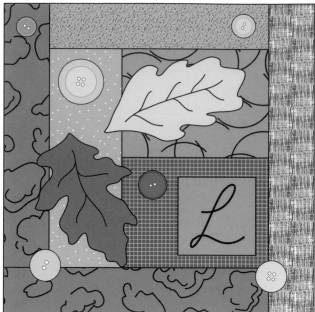

L is for Leaf Cutting Plan

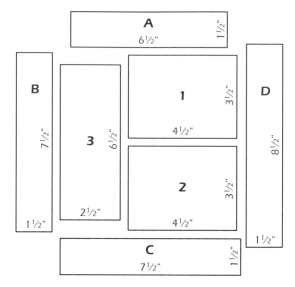

The measurements shown include ¼"-wide seam allowances.

Cut 1

Cut 1

Cut 1

1. Using a transfer pen, transfer the veins of the leaves to your leaf appliqué pieces. Follow the pen manufacturer's instructions.
2. Referring to the block illustration for placement, position the leaves on the block and embroider the veins on the leaves. See "Using Embroidery" on page 11.
3. Stitch the *L* on a 2" square of fabric, then stitch the square of fabric to the block.

M is for Milk

M is for Milk Cutting Plan

Color photo on page 44

	D 8½"	1½"	
C 7½"	1 6½"	2 6½"	3 6½"	A 6½"
1½"	2½"	2½"	2½"	1½"

| B1 3½" | 1½" | B2 4½" | ½" |

The measurements shown include ¼"-wide seam allowances.

1
Cut 1

MILK

2 → Cut 1

Embroider edge of glass

1. Using a transfer pen, transfer the word "MILK" to the milk bottle appliqué piece. Follow the pen manufacturer's instructions. I used a permanent-ink fabric marking pen to write on my Alphabet block. You can use this technique or embroider the letters on the appliqué piece.

2. Transfer the outline of the glass to the background as described in step 1. Refer to the block illustration for placement. Embroider the outline of the glass using a backstitch.

3. For the milk bottle and the milk in the glass, cut one appliqué piece from muslin and a second appliqué piece from white flannel. Cut the flannel pieces slightly smaller than the muslin pieces. Layer the pieces, muslin on top, and stitch to the block. The flannel prevents the background fabric from showing through the muslin.

The cinnamon cookie buttons are from Sugar Babies. See "Resources" on page 21.

Color photo on page 44

M is for Muffin Cutting Plan

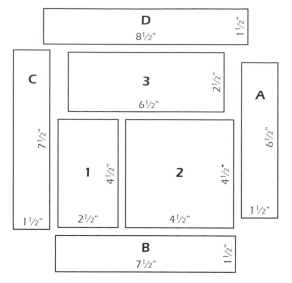

The measurements shown include ¼"-wide seam allowances.

Refer to the block illustration for placement. Sew small beads to the muffin tops. I used blue wooden beads for blueberries.

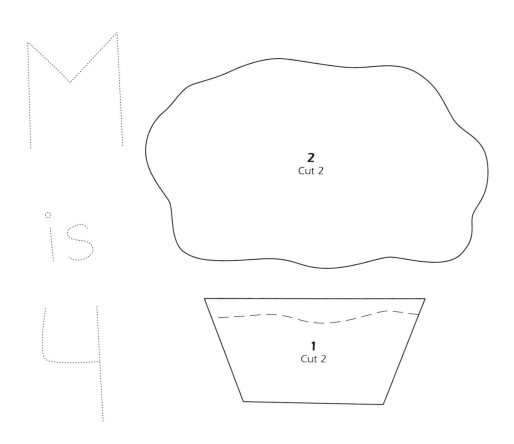

2 Cut 2

1 Cut 2

Color
photo
on page
44

N is for Needle Cutting Plan

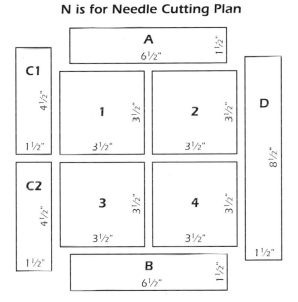

The measurements shown include ¼"-wide seam allowances.

1. Cut the "eye" out of the needle with small, straight scissors.
2. With a contrasting color of embroidery floss or perle cotton, make a few large stitches on the block. End your stitching where the eye of the needle will lie. Leave a long tail.
3. Thread the tail through the eye of the needle piece before stitching it in place.

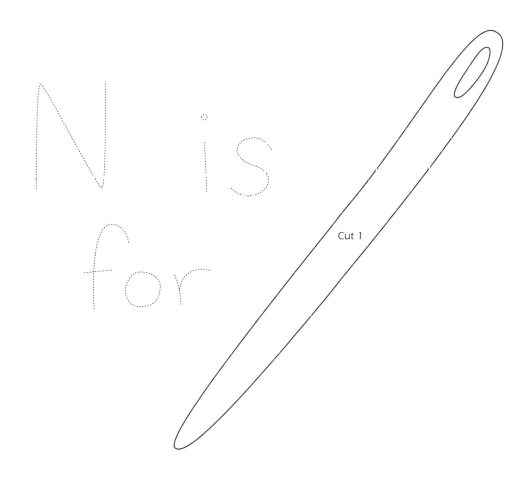

Cut 1

Color
photo
on page
44

N is for Nest Cutting Plan

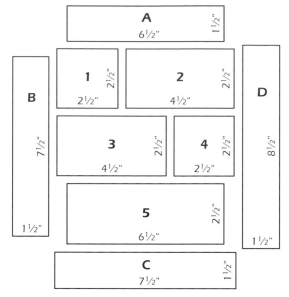

The measurements shown include ¼"-wide seam allowances.

Cut 1

P is for Patterns

Refer to the block illustration for placement. I purchased the nest and eggs at a local craft supply shop. I glued the eggs in the nest, then stitched the nest to the block, tying off on the back.

The birdhouse pin is from Ann Shafer. See "Resources" on page 21.

O is for Oatmeal Cutting Plan

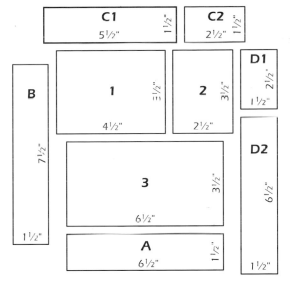

Color photo on page 65

The measurements shown include ¼"-wide seam allowances.

1. Referring to the block illustration for placement, stitch the bowl and spoon on the block.
2. Using a transfer pen, transfer the steam lines to the background. Follow the pen manufacturer's instructions. Embroider the steam lines with three strands of embroidery floss.

I found the milk bottles and basket in a craft supply shop that carries miniatures.

Color
photo
on page
65

O is for Orange Cutting Plan

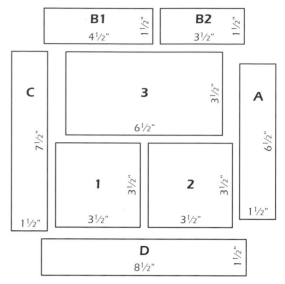

The measurements shown include ¼"-wide seam allowances.

Use a black permanent-ink fabric marker to make the navel lines. Refer to the block illustration and template for placement.

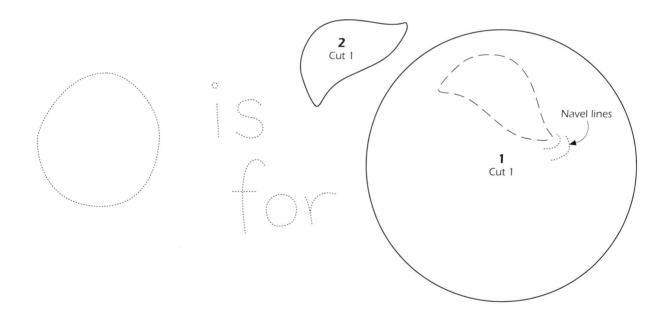

2
Cut 1

Navel lines

1
Cut 1

P is for Pie

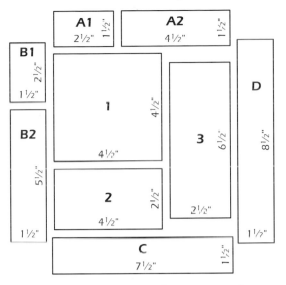

P is for Pie Cutting Plan

A1 2½" 1½"	A2 4½" 1½"	
B1 2½" 1½"	1 4½" 4½"	D 8½"
B2 5½" 1½"	3 6½" 2½"	
	2 4½" 2½"	1½"
	C 7½" 1½"	

The measurements shown include ¼"-wide seam allowances.

1. Referring to the block illustration for placement, stitch the pie pan and crust pieces to the block.

2. Using a transfer pen, transfer the steam lines to the background. Follow the pen manufacturer's instructions. Embroider the steam lines using three strands of embroidery floss. The red apple button is available at most fabric stores.

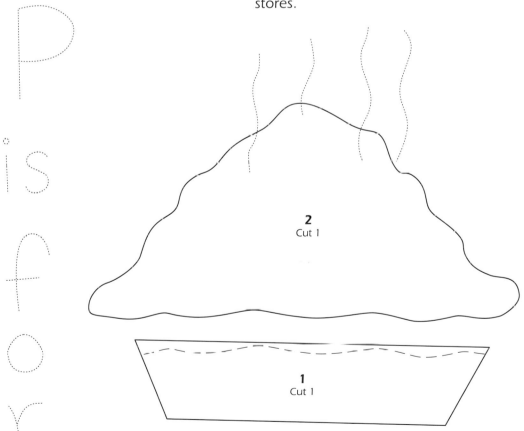

2
Cut 1

1
Cut 1

Color
photo
on page
65

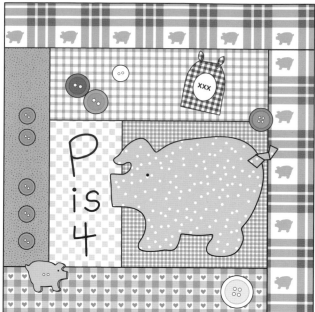

P is for Pig Cutting Plan

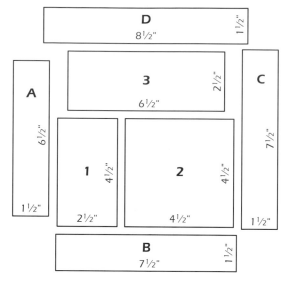

The measurements shown include ¼"-wide seam allowances.

1. Using pinking shears, cut a ¼" x 1" fabric strip for the pig's tail.
2. Referring to the block illustration and template for placement, stitch the tail to the pig and secure with a square knot. Twist the fabric strip and secure the free end on the block with another square knot.

I purchased the feed bag and pig button at a local craft supply shop.

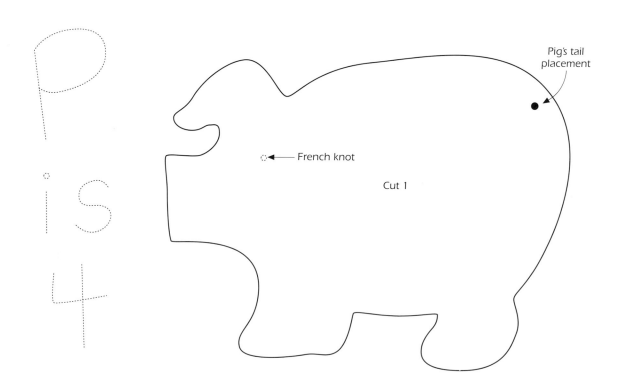

Pig's tail placement

French knot

Cut 1

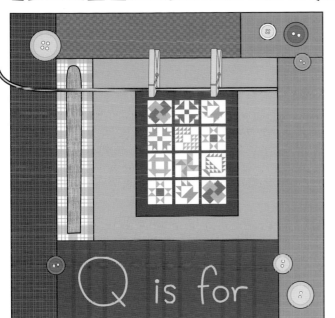

Q is for Quilt Cutting Plan

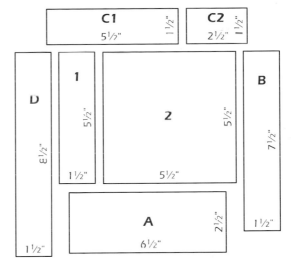

Color
photo
on page
65

The measurements shown include ¼"-wide seam allowances.

To make the quilt top, I stenciled the little blocks on muslin, but you could also use "cheater" cloth or small prints to make a miniature quilt.

1. The finished size of the quilt is 2¾" x 3½". Using pinking shears or the pinking blade of your rotary cutter, cut a 3¼" x 4" rectangle of black fabric.

2. Cut a 2¾" x 3½" rectangle of muslin. Stencil or draw little quilt blocks on the muslin. I used a small stencil brush and red and blue stamp pads. Use a black permanent-ink fabric marker to make the lines between the blocks.

3. Place the muslin on top of the black fabric and turn the edges of the black fabric over the muslin. Stitch the edges in place with perle cotton or embroidery floss. Press well.

4. Cut a 9"-long piece of jute. Referring to the block illustration for placement, position the piece of jute and two small clothespins on the block.

5. Using invisible nylon thread and a zigzag stitch, machine stitch the piece of jute to the block. Do not stitch the areas covered by the clothespins.

6. Trim the jute, if necessary, and clip the little quilt to the block with the clothespins.

The clothespins are available in most craft supply shops. The quilt block stencil is from Country Stencils. See "Resources" on page 21.

Cut 1

Color photo on page 65

R is for Radish Cutting Plan

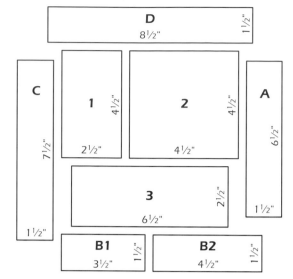

D 8½"			1½"

C 7½"	**1** 4½"	**2** 4½"	**A** 6½"
1½"	2½"	4½"	1½"

3 6½"	2½"

B1 3½"	1½"	**B2** 4½"	1½"

The measurements shown include ¼"-wide seam allowances.

Refer to the block illustration for placement. I received the radish seed-packet button as a gift. Seed-packet buttons are available from Apple Creek. See "Resources" on page 21.

R is for

2
Cut 1

1
Cut 1

3
Cut 1

R is for Rainbow

Color
photo
on page
66

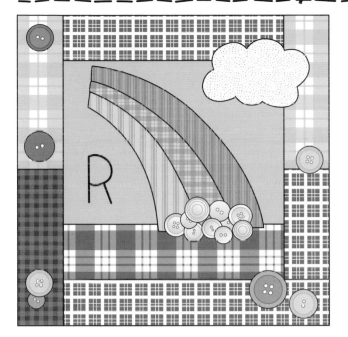

R is for Rainbow Cutting Plan

D1		A		B1
4½"		6½"	1½"	4½"
1½"				1½"

	1			
		5"		

D2				B2
4½"		6½"		3½"
1½"				1½"

	2		
	6½"	2"	

C	
7½"	1½"

The measurements shown include ¼"-wide seam allowances.

Use contrasting fabrics for the rainbow. Cut the appliqué pieces slightly larger than drawn so you can overlap them. Refer to the block illustration for placement.

I sewed assorted metallic gold buttons at the end of the rainbow.

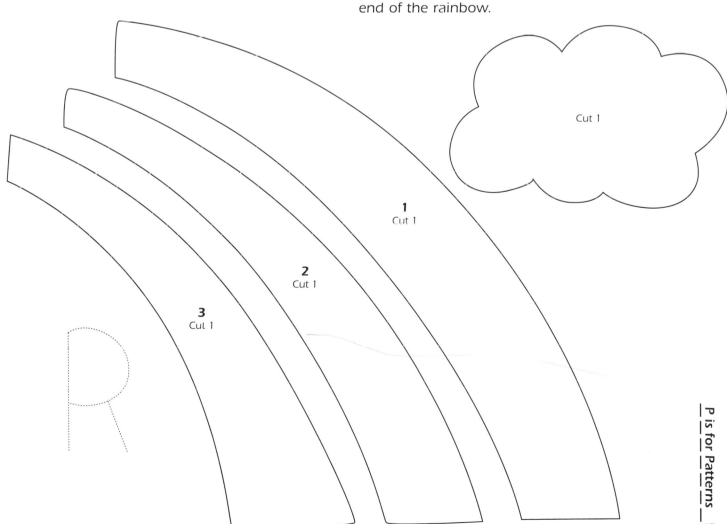

1
Cut 1

2
Cut 1

3
Cut 1

Cut 1

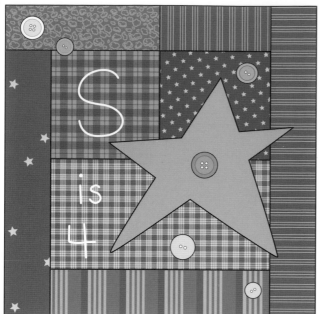

Color
photo
on page
66

S is for Star Cutting Plan

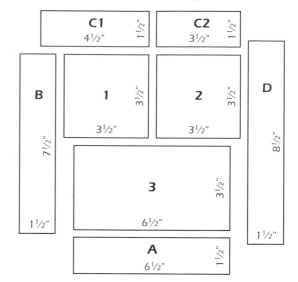

C1		C2	
4½"	1½"	3½"	1½"

B	1	2	D
7½"	3½"	3½"	8½"
	3½"	3½"	

3
3½"
6½"

A
6½"   1½"

B: 1½"   D: 1½"

The measurements shown include ¼"-wide seam allowances.

There are no special instructions for this Alphabet block. Refer to the block illustration for placement.

Cut 1

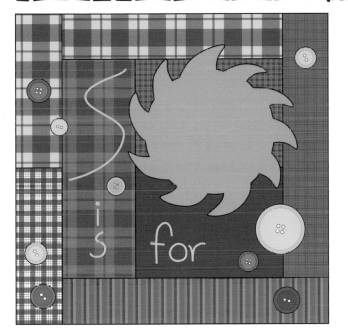

S is for Sun Cutting Plan

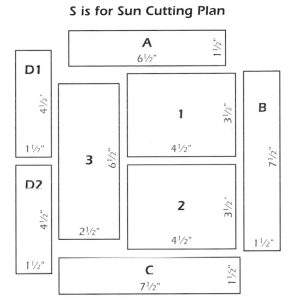

Color photo on page 66

The measurements shown include ¼"-wide seam allowances.

There are no special instructions for this Alphabet block. Refer to the block illustration for placement.

Cut 1

Color
photo
on page
66

T is for Teapot Cutting Plan

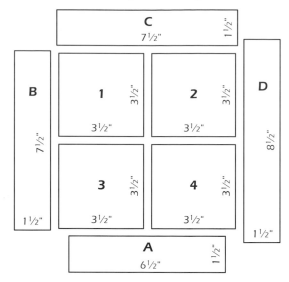

The measurements shown include ¼"-wide seam allowances.

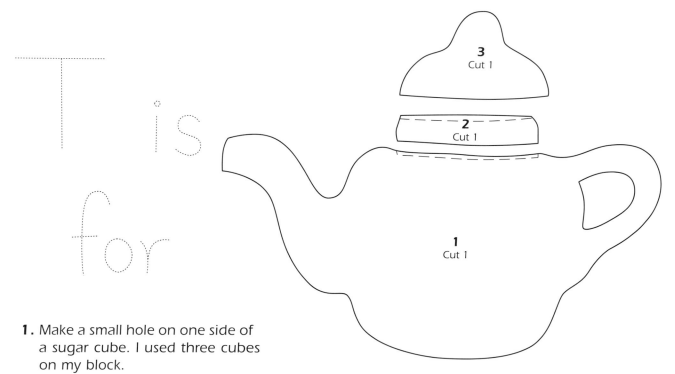

1. Make a small hole on one side of a sugar cube. I used three cubes on my block.

2. Cut a 6"-long piece of perle cotton or embroidery floss (use all six strands). Using an epoxy glue that will not melt, attach one end of the perle cotton or embroidery floss to the sugar cube. Allow plenty of time for the glue to dry.

3. Melt paraffin wax, following the manufacturer's instructions. Dip the sugar cube into the melted wax three or four times, allowing the wax to soak in well after each coating. Allow to dry.

4. Thread a needle with the other end of the perle cotton or embroidery floss. Position a button on the block and stitch the button and cubes in place. Refer to the block illustration for placement.

5. I recommend that you use a solid fabric for the appliqué piece between the teapot and lid. This helps define the shapes of the teapot and lid.

The blue heart button is from Dogwood Lane. See "Resources" on page 21.

T is for Tomato

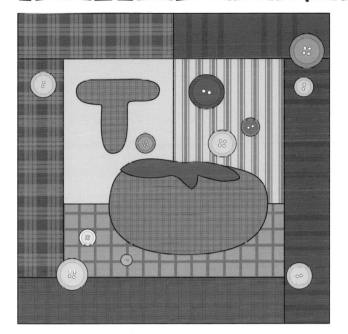

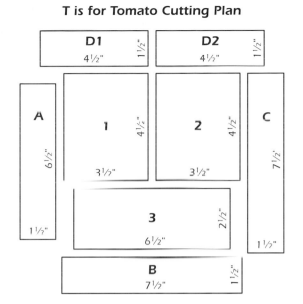

T is for Tomato Cutting Plan

Color photo on page 66

D1 4½"	1½"	D2 4½"	1½"

A — 6½" — 1½"

1 — 4½" — 3½"

2 — 4½" — 3½"

C — 7½" — 1½"

3 — 6½" — 2½"

B — 7½" — 1½"

The measurements shown include ¼"-wide seam allowances.

There are no special instructions for this Alphabet block. Refer to the block illustration for placement.

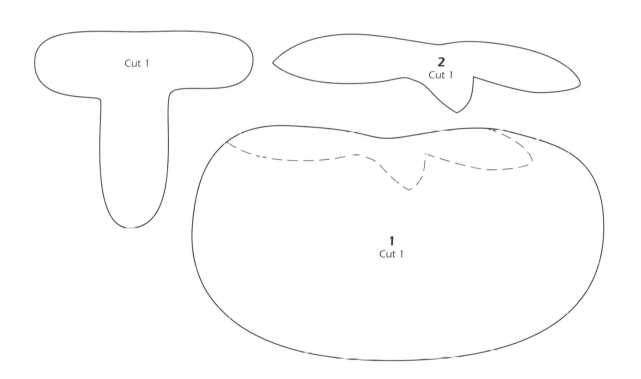

Cut 1

2
Cut 1

1
Cut 1

Color
photo
on page
66

U is for Umbrella Cutting Plan

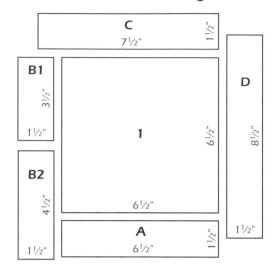

The measurements shown include ¼"-wide seam allowances.

1. Cut the umbrella sections slightly larger than drawn so you can overlap them.

2. Using a transfer pen, transfer the rain lines to the background. Follow the pen manufacturer's instructions.

3. Referring to the block illustration for placement, position the umbrella on the block and embroider the rain lines.

V is for Vase

V is for Vase Cutting Plan

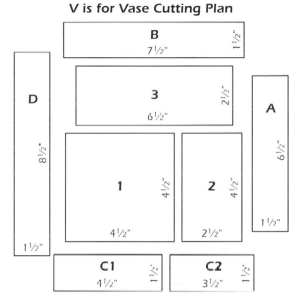

The measurements shown include ¼"-wide seam allowances.

1. Make the yo-yos as described on page 12. Refer to the block illustration for placement.
2. Using a transfer pen, transfer the flower stems to the background. Follow the pen manufacturer's instruction. Embroider the stems on the block.

The small wooden heart button is available at most craft supply shops.

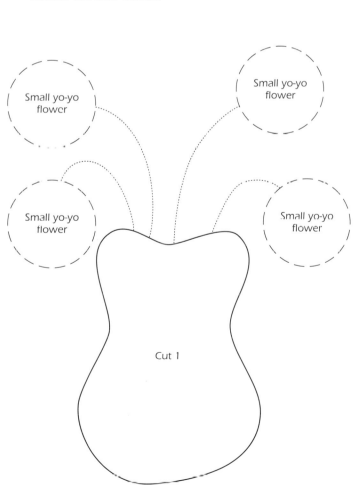

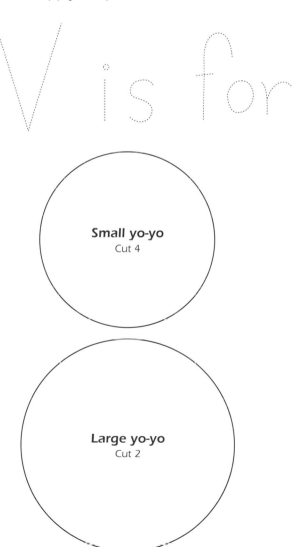

Color
photo
on page
67

W is for Window Cutting Plan

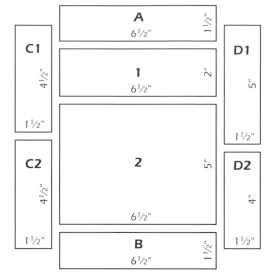

The measurements shown include ¼"-wide seam allowances.

1. Using a transfer pen, transfer the window lines onto the appliqué pieces. Follow the pen manufacturer's instructions.

2. Position the appliqué pieces on the block, referring to the block illustration for placement. Embroider the windowpanes, stitching through all the layers of the block. See "Using Embroidery" on page 11.

3. Using pinking shears or the pinking blade of a rotary cutter, cut two 1" x 4½" pieces of fabric.

4. Cut a comfortable length of perle cotton or embroidery floss. Tie a knot in one end, leaving a 6"-long tail. Stitch along the 4½"-long edge, approximately ¼" from the top.

5. Gather the stitches slightly and adjust the valance to fit the top of a window. Pin in place. Do not remove the perle cotton or floss from the needle.

6. Stitch the valance to the window. Tie the ends of the perle cotton or embroidery floss in a square knot and trim. Repeat this procedure for the second valance.

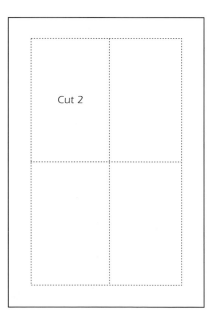

Cut 2

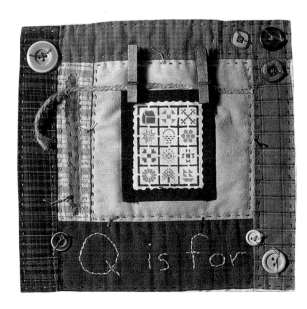

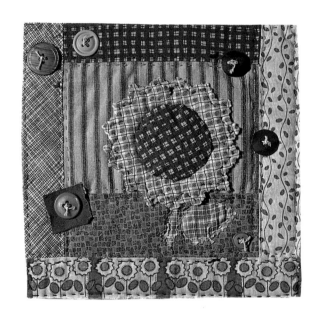

X is for X-Stitch Cutting Plan

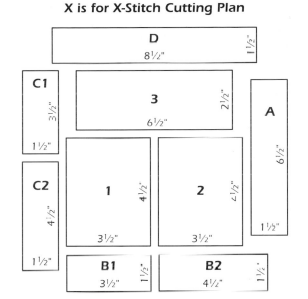

The measurements shown include ¼"-wide seam allowances.

Color photo on page 67

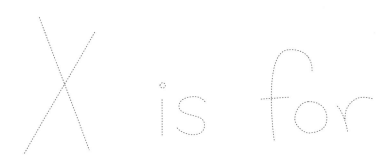

Embroider or draw the design of your choice. Initials make a nice gift.

1. To cross-stitch a design for the embroidery hoop, cut a 4" square of Aida fabric. I used a 3"-wide hoop for my block. If your hoop is a different size, cut the square of Aida 1" larger than the size of your hoop. Cross-stitch your design. You can also cut a 4" square of muslin and mark small Xs in the shape of a design or letter with a permanent-ink fabric marker.

2. Referring to the block illustration for placement, attach the loose corners of the Aida fabric to the block with buttons.

3. Thread a tapestry needle with a short length of embroidery floss. Place it through the fabric in the hoop.

4. Rewind a partial skein of embroidery floss, making loops approximately 4" long. Replace the paper label. Working from the back of the block, stitch the skein in place.

Miniature needlework hoops are available at most needlework shops.

Color
photo
on page
67

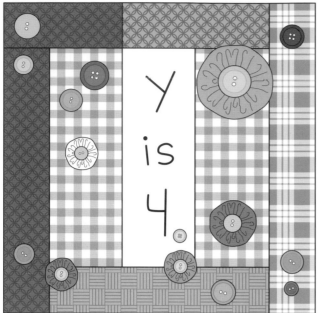

Y is for Yo-Yo Cutting Plan

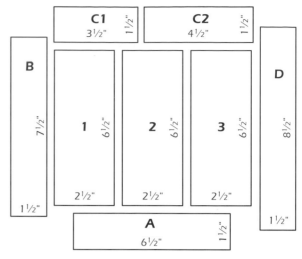

The measurements shown include ¼"-wide seam allowances.

Make yo-yos as described on page 12. Make
as many yo-yos as you want. I used one large,
one medium and three small yo-yos.

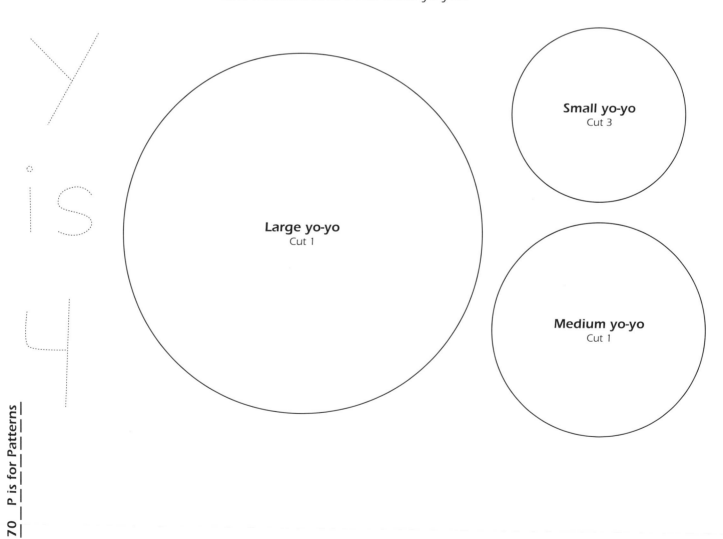

Small yo-yo
Cut 3

Large yo-yo
Cut 1

Medium yo-yo
Cut 1

Color
photo
on page
67

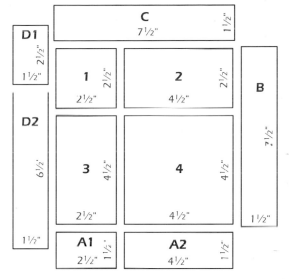

Z is for Zipper Cutting Plan

			C 7½" 1½"		
D1 2½" 1½"	1 2½" 2½"	2 4½" 2½"			B 7½" 1½"
D2 6½' 1½"	3 2½" 4½"	4 4½" 4½"			
	A1 2½" 1½'	A2 4½" 1½"			

The measurements shown include ¼"-wide seam allowances.

Machine stitch zippers to the block. Use as
many zippers as you want.

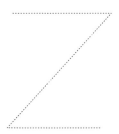

Daisies

Daisies Spacer Block Cutting Plan

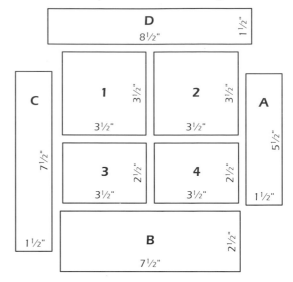

D		
8½"		1½"

C	1	2	A
7½"	3½" / 3½"	3½" / 3½"	5½"
	3	4	
	2½" / 3½"	2½" / 3½"	1½"
1½"	B		
	7½"	2½"	

The measurements shown include ¼"-wide seam allowances.

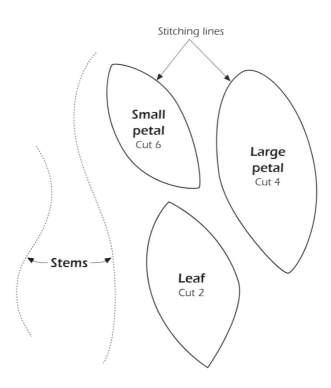

Stitching lines

Small
petal
Cut 6

Large
petal
Cut 4

Stems

Leaf
Cut 2

1. Cut 1 rectangle of backing fabric and 1 rectangle of fusible fleece, each 3" x 12". I used muslin for my backing fabric. Fuse the backing fabric to the fleece, following the fleece manufacturer's instructions.

2. For the daisy petals, cut another rectangle, also 3" x 12", of muslin. Trace around the petal templates on the right side of the muslin. Do not cut out the petals.

3. Pin this piece of muslin to the fused background, with the marked side facing up. Using yellow perle cotton or embroidery floss, stitch around the petals. Stitch through all the layers. Using pinking shears, cut the petals out ⅛" to ¼" from the stitching.

4. Using a transfer pen, transfer the flower stems to the background. Follow the pen manufacturer's instructions. Embroider the flower stems on the block. Stitch a leaf at the base of each stem.

5. Referring to the illustration, position the petals on the block and stitch large yellow buttons to hold the petals in place. Tie off on the top of the block.

Spool Spacer Block Cutting Plan

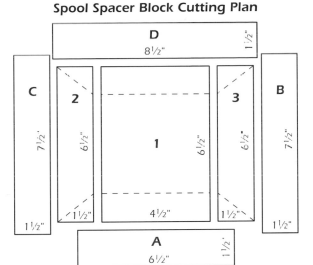

		D
		8½" 1½"

C 7½"   2 6½"   1 6½" 6½"   3 6½"   B 7½"

1½"   1½"   4½"   1½"   1½"

A 6½" 1½"

The measurements shown include ¼"-wide seam allowances.

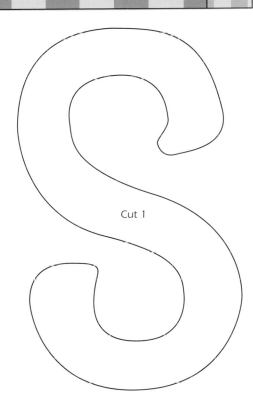

Cut 1

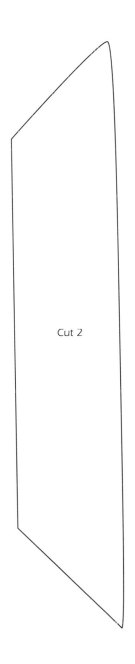

Cut 2

Use this as a quilt label, Initial block, or Alphabet block.

Piece the block, then position and stitch the top and bottom of the spool as shown in the block illustration, If making a label, in the center of the spool, write your name, location (your full address or just your city), and the date you made the quilt or gave it as a gift. If it is a gift, include the occasion and recipient.

If making an Alphabet block, stitch the letter *S* in the spool. If you want an Initial block, stitch the appropriate letter in place of the *S*.

Sunflower

Color
photo
on page
68

Sunflower Spacer Block Cutting Plan

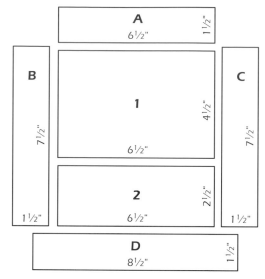

The measurements shown include ¼"-wide seam allowances.

1. Stitch the stem and leaf in place. Refer to the block illustration for placement.

2. Cut 1 square of muslin and 1 square of fusible fleece, each 5" x 5". Fuse the muslin to the fleece, following the fleece manufacturer's instructions.

3. Cut a 5" square of the sunflower fabric. Trace around the template on the right side of the fabric. Do not cut out the sunflower.

4. Pin the 5" square of sunflower fabric to the fused background, marked side facing up. Stitch around the edges on the drawn line. Stitch through all the layers. Using pinking shears, cut the sunflower out ⅛" to ¼" from the stitching.

5. Make a yo-yo as described on page 12. Place the yo-yo in the middle of the flower, smooth side facing up. Pin in place.

6. Blindstitch the edge of the yo-yo to the center of the sunflower. Attach the sunflower by taking several stitches from the back side of the block.

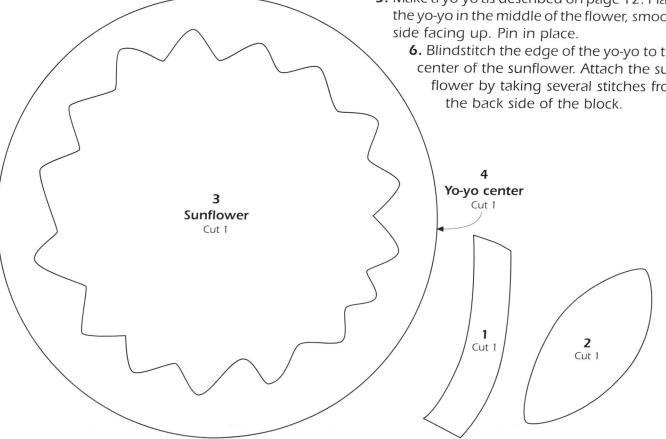

3
Sunflower
Cut 1

4
Yo-yo center
Cut 1

1
Cut 1

2
Cut 1

74   P is for Patterns

Yo-Yo Flower

Flower Spacer Block Cutting Plan

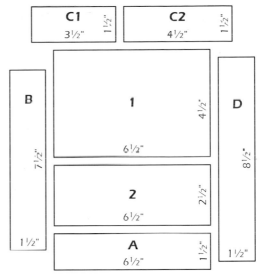

The measurements shown include ¼"-wide seam allowances.

1. Stitch the stems and leaves in place. Refer to the block illustration for placement.
2. Make yo-yos as described on page 12. Each flower is made of 2 yo-yos, one large and one small.
3. To make the left flower, position the larger yo-yo over the stem, smooth side up. Pin in place.
4. Working from the back of the block, blindstitch the yo-yo in place. Stitch through all the layers. Tie off on the back of the block.
5. Place the smaller yo-yo in the middle of the flower, gathered side facing

up. Sew a button through the center of the yo-yo to secure.
6. To make the right flower, repeat steps 3 and 4, but place the large yo-yo gathered side up.
7. Place the smaller yo-yo in the middle of the flower, gathered side down, and blindstitch the edges to the large yo-yo.

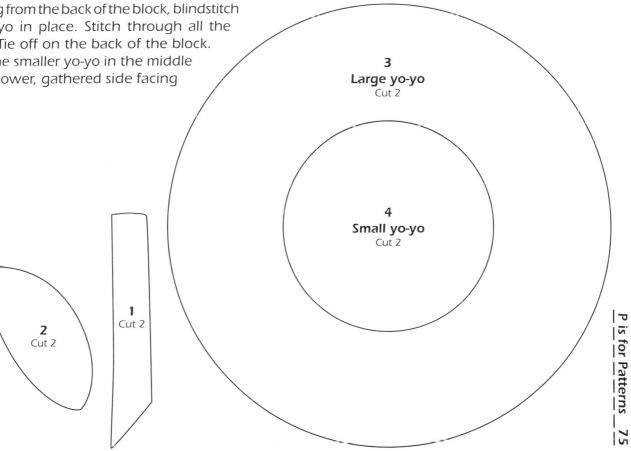

Color
photos
on page
68

1. With pinking shears or a rotary cutter, cut one 4" x 6" rectangle each from the background fabric, the fusible fleece, and the backing fabric.

2. If you are making the Good For You block, transfer the lettering to the 2½" x 4¾" background appliqué piece (page 77). Use a transfer pen and follow the pen manufacturer's instructions. Embroider the lettering with embroidery floss.

If you are making the Happy Birthday block, transfer the letters to the ¾" x 2" and ¾" x 3½" cake appliqué pieces, and the candles to the background. Embroider the letters and candles.

If you are making the House block, trace, cut, and appliquilt the letters and the 2½" x 4¾" background piece to the block.

3. Fuse the backing fabric to the fusible fleece, following the fleece manufacturer's instructions. The fusible fleece provides stiffness and helps the block to lie flat against the border. If you use white or light-colored fabric to make the cake on the Happy Birthday block, you may want to fuse fleece to the back of the appliqué pieces. The fleece prevents the background fabric from showing through the appliqué piece.

4. Stitch the appliqué pieces to the blocks. Stitch through all the layers.

5. Sew buttons to the top corners of the block. Attach pieces of ribbon, jute, or the tie of your choice with buttons. Estimate the length to fit your button foundation.

GOOD

FOR YOU

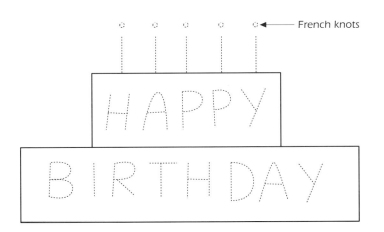

← French knots

HAPPY

BIRTHDAY

THE

Now I Know My A Bee Zzzz

I divided this quilt into three sections and used the "quilt-as-you-go" method I devised and teach. Dividing the quilt into sections makes it much easier to handle and to stitch. It also adds an opportunity to be creative when choosing the background. I chose three different fabrics, all of the same value. I would caution you not to use fabrics that are too bright or busy, as they may compete with the blocks. Stitch the pieced blocks directly onto the backgrounds. When all three sections are finished, assemble the quilt and add the borders and binding.

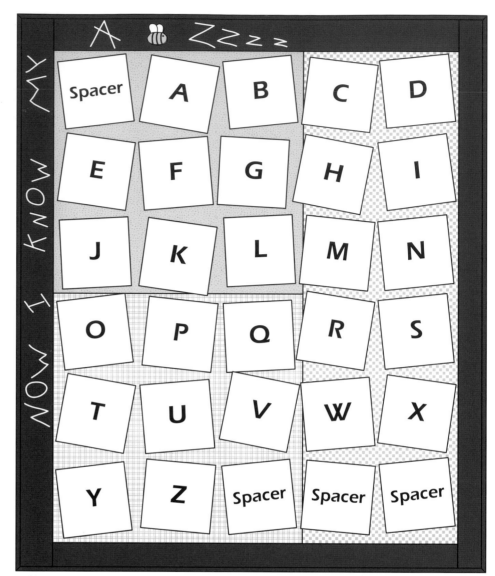

Color Photo: page 17
Size: 62" x 54"
Materials: 44"-wide fabric

⅞ yd. beige print for Background 1

¾ yd. beige plaid for Background 2

1⅝ yds. beige check for Background 3*

1 yd. black for borders and binding

3 yds. dark print for backing

3 yds. Pellon fleece or other thin batting

Scraps for each block

Bee buttons (See "Resources" on page 21)

*For a whole-cloth background, cut one long piece from the 1⅝ yards. If you prefer, you can piece the background from ⅞ yard.

Cutting

From the beige print, cut:
    1 square, 29¾" x 29¾",
    for Background 1

From the beige plaid, cut:
    1 rectangle, 26¾" x 29¾",
    for Background 2

From the beige check, cut:
    1 rectangle, 18¾" x 55¼",
    for Background 3

From the black border fabric, cut:
    1 strip, 4½" x 56", for the top border
    1 strip, 3½" x 56", for the bottom border
    1 strip, 4½" x 55½", for the left border
    1 strip, 3½" x 55½", for the right border

From the dark print, cut:
    1 square, 36" x 36", for Backing 1
    1 square, 36" x 36", for Backing 2
    1 rectangle, 22" x 62", for Backing 3

From the Pellon fleece, cut:
    1 square, 35" x 35", for Batting 1
    1 square, 31" x 35", for Batting 2
    1 rectangle, 21" x 62", for Batting 3

Assembly

All seam allowances are ¼" wide.

1. Layer the background, batting, and backing for each section. The cut measurements for the backing include ½" that will extend beyond the batting where sections are joined and a ¼"-wide seam allowance for the borders.

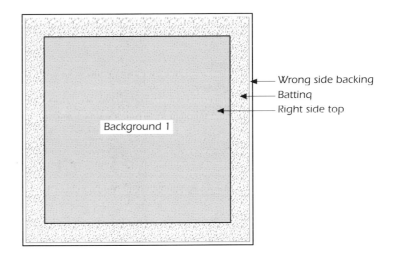

Wrong side backing
Batting
Right side top

2. Piece the tops of your Alphabet and Spacer blocks.
3. Referring to the quilt illustration for placement, pin a spacer block and blocks A, B, E, F, G, J, K, and L to Background 1. Smooth the background from the center to the outside edges as you pin. Pin the appliqué pieces in place on the blocks. I placed my blocks in a crooked fashion; some overlap the seams between the background pieces.

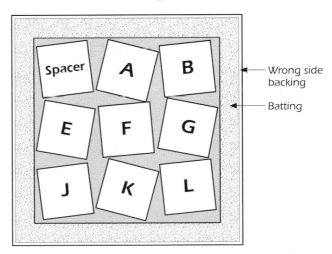

Wrong side backing

Batting

4. Using your needle, turn under the raw edges on each block ¼". Stitch through all the layers. (Or pink the edges of each block, then stitch them to the quilt sandwich without turning under the raw edges.)

5. Appliquilt the pieced blocks to the background, stitching through all the layers. If you put blocks near the edges, do not stitch them until after you join the background pieces. Embellish the blocks.

6. Repeating steps 2–5, stitch blocks O, P, Q, T, U, V, Y, Z, and a spacer block to Background 2. Stitch blocks C, D, H, I, M, N, R, S, W, X, and two spacer blocks to Background 3.

7. Pin the background and backing fabrics away from the lower edge of Background 1 and the top edge of Background 2, exposing the batting.

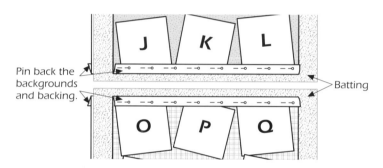

Butt the lower edge of the Background 1 batting to the upper edge of the Background 2 batting. Do not overlap. Using a wide zigzag stitch, machine stitch the edges together. Position the edges together as you go. You want to come to the end of each piece of batting at the same time. Ease as necessary. When you reach the end of the batting, make sure that you have not left any "holes" in your stitching. Repair any holes and remove the pins.

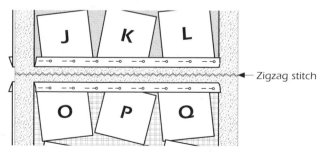

8. Turn the quilt over to the back. Smooth one piece of backing fabric over the seam in the batting. Place the other piece of backing fabric on top and turn under the raw edge. Pin in place. Using a blind hem or other decorative stitch, stitch the edge of the backing fabric in place. Do not stitch through all the layers.

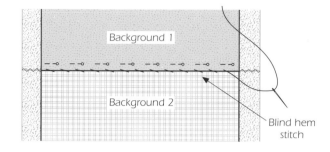

9. Turn the quilt over to the front. Remove the pins from the background fabric. Smooth one piece of background fabric over the seam in the batting. Place the other piece of background fabric on top and turn under the raw edge. Pin in place. I used perle cotton and a cross-stitch to stitch this seam down. You may want to use a blind hem or other decorative stitch. You can sew by hand or machine.

10. Finish stitching any blocks left unfinished along the upper and lower edges of Backgrounds 1 and 2.

11. Repeating steps 7–10, attach Background 3 along the right edge of Backgrounds 1 and 2.

Finishing

1. Your completed background should measure approximately 46½" x 55". This measurement does not include the batting and backing, which should extend beyond the background for your borders. If your piece does not exactly match these measurements, do not worry. As long as all the blocks are attached and the opposing edges are the same measurement, it's fine. If the opposing sides are not equal, trim so they match in length. This ensures that your quilt will hang evenly.

2. Place the right and left borders on top of the completed background, right sides together, matching the raw edges. You may need to trim the border strips if you trimmed your background. Pin in place. Using a ¼"-wide seam allowance, machine stitch through all the layers.

Flip the borders right side up onto the batting. Press the seams. Repeat the procedure for the top and bottom borders. Trim the excess batting and backing fabric even with the border edges.

3. Bind the quilt. I used a traditional binding for this quilt, but the appliquilt binding on page 16 also works well.

4. Using a white transfer pen, transfer the lettering on pages 82–83 to the border. Follow the pen manufacturer's directions. Using 3 strands of embroidery floss and a backstitch or stem stitch, embroider the lettering. See "Using Embroidery" on page 11.

5. Stitch the bee buttons in place. Refer to the quilt photo for placement.

6. Using a running stitch and contrasting embroidery floss or perle cotton, stitch between blocks to resemble the flight path of the bees.

7. Be sure to make a label for your quilt.

Using a photocopy machine, enlarge the lettering on pages 82 and 83 by 125% to make it the correct size for your quilt.

Use button or embroider.

That Patchwork Place Publications and Products